GAIN
A BETTER BRAIN

How to Retrain Your Brain to Learn
Anything Faster, Unleash Its Full Potential
and Keep Your Mind Sharp at Any Age

PETER POWELL

Copyright © 2021 by Peter Powell.
All rights reserved.

No part of this book may be reproduced in any form on by any electronic or mechanical means, including information storage and retrieval systems, without permission in writing from the publisher, except by a reviewer who may quote brief passages in a review.

Book and Cover design: Raphael A.
Printed in the United States of America

First Edition : February, 2021

CONTENTS

Introduction 1
Chapter one – Know Your Brain 4
Chapter two – Maintaining Memory 18
Chapter three – Concentration 30
Chapter four – Self-Learning 43
Chapter five – Accelerated Learning And Speed Reading 61
Conclusion 81

INTRODUCTION

Throughout life, all the body's organs disintegrate and lose their capacity to play out their capacities ideally, particularly the mind. For this reason, many people are adopting habits to stay in shape and prevent their quality of life from deteriorating in the long term.

However, few pay enough attention to their mental health. And it is usually one of the most affected in old age. If not trained, it can lead to several mental problems, memory loss, or difficulty sleeping.
Good habits in youth and maturity are one of the keys to generating resistance to neurodegenerative diseases.

But being aware of the importance of all this in the long term is not our strength.

Bad habits in middle age can have serious repercussions decades later, generating cerebrovascular problems or increasing the risk of dementia.
The brain is everything. We are our brains. When our brain fails, it is called brain death. The scientific community has accepted that when the brain stops working irreversibly, the subject has died. It is the fundamental part that makes us human beings or independent individuals, and therefore, it is essential to take care of it.

In our genome, we have programmed a series of functions for the activities or events around us. But evolution invented a system that was adaptable to the circumstances that exist. If a predator appears, the subject was able to recognize it and flee or hunt it down. It is an evolutionary invention. The nervous system has managed to reach the civilization of the human being.

You can have a great brain and cognitive function despite the passage of time. It is possible, thanks to the adoption of good habits.

To make your brain work, you have to know it well. When you know how it works, you will develop activities to keep your brain in shape. Also, it is a process that involves concentration, self-learning, etc. It is all that you are going to see in this book. Take a little time to read it. In this book, you will discover a secret about how to train your brain, which is like any other body part, to get it in shape.

Enjoy it!

CHAPTER ONE

KNOW YOUR BRAIN

The brain is perhaps the most intricate organs in the human body. Additionally, it is quite possibly the most significant. It is part of the encephalon, which together, with the spinal cord, constitute the central nervous system.

The encephalon controls and regulates the vital functions of the human body. Thanks to it, the body performs the functions for its survival.

In humans, the brain is responsible for higher mental or cognitive functions. Focus, memory, reasoning, thought, character and language are the qualities that make people outstanding.

In the learning process, the brain plays a fundamental role. It is a process that carries out on three levels, present throughout life but especially important in childhood:

- Sensory perception
- The encoding and decoding of messages
- Higher or abstract thinking

When you know how your brain and how it relates to the outside world, it is the key to improve or perfect learning in humans.

Nine things you should know about your brain

1. If we were to place all the neurons of an adult brain (100,000 million) in a single file, they would occupy approximately 1,000 kilometers.

2. The human brain weighs 1,400 grams, and around 25% of the calories we consume daily destine to "feed" it. The giraffe's brain weighs about half that, 680 grams; 420 grams that of a chimpanzee; 6,000 grams that of an elephant; and only 7.6 that of a squirrel.

3. While we are awake, our brain consumes an amount of electricity equivalent to what is needed to illuminate a low-voltage light bulb (25 watts).

4. The process of recognizing a face start in the brain. First, the brain looks person at the eyes, and then at the shape of the mouth and nose.

5. There is a protein called RGS-14 that increases visual memory up to 1,500 times. It could become a good ally for students of any age.

6. The life expectancy of a neuron of the sense of smell is only sixty days. After that time, it replaces by a new one. Despite this ongoing recycling, our memory for odors is unbeatable. What is more, the smell is the sense with the considerable capacity to awaken sleeping memories.

7. The key to prejudice is also in our brain. While thinking about like-minded people sets in motion the central area of the medial prefrontal cortex, the dorsal area is activated when we think of those who have opinions different from ours.

8. Eating a Mediterranean diet can protect the brain from injuries relate to small strokes, as Nikolaos Scarmeas of Columbia University has recently shown (USA.). Scarmeas has also proven that this diet reduces the risk of Alzheimer's disease.

9. The adult brain continues to generate neurons throughout life. The process is known as neurogenesis,

and it occurs mainly in the hippocampus, a brain region linked to memory and learning. Doing aerobics physical exercise, for example jogging, stimulates neurogenesis.

Neural diseases

The mind, spinal line, and nerves form the sensory system of humans. They are both, in charge of all the elements of the body. If there is an anomaly in one part of your nervous system, you can experience difficulty in moving, speaking, swallowing, breathing, or learning. There may likewise be issues with memory, detects, or disposition.

There is a vast of them, more than 600. The most recognized types include:

1. Those that are results of of missing of genes: _Huntington's disease_ and _muscular dystrophy_

☐ _Huntington's disease_

Huntington's disease is an inherited disease that causes the breakdown of some nerve cells in the brain. People are born with the defective gene, but symptoms do not appear until after their 30s or 40s. The initial symptoms of this disease can include uncontrolled movements, clumsiness, and balance problems. Later, it may prevent walking, talking, and swallowing. Some people stop recognizing their family members. Others are aware of their surroundings and can express their emotions.

There is no cure. Some medicines can help you control some symptoms, but they cannot slow or stop the disease.

☐ *Muscular dystrophy*

That infection cause muscle shortcoming and loss of mass. A few dystrophies show up in outset or adolescence; others don't show up later. The various sorts fluctuate contingent upon who they influence and the indications. All types of solid dystrophy deteriorate as the muscles debilitate, and a great many people with this condition at some point or another lose the capacity to move.

Its treatment has not been developed, but doctors can control the symptoms and avoid deteriorations.

2. Problems with the development of the nervous system, such as *spina bifida*

☐ *Spina bifida*

It is a neural tube defect, a type of birth problem of the brain, spine, or spinal cord. That defect appears when the spine of the fetus does not close completely during the first month of pregnancy. That can harm the nerves and spinal line. Screening tests during pregnancy can diagnose spina bifida. Now and then it is found after the infant is conceived.

The indications of spina bifida differ from individual to individual. Most people with spina bifida have usual intelligence. Others need assistive devices, such as braces, crutches, or wheelchairs.

The exact cause of spina bifida is unknown, although it seems to run in families. Taking folic corrosive can diminish the danger of having an infant with spina bifida. And it can find in most multivitamin supplements. Ladies who can get pregnant should take it every day.

3. *Degenerative diseases*, in which nerve cells are damaged or die, such as *Parkinson's disease* and *Alzheimer's disease*

- *Neurodegenerative diseases*

Other names: Degenerative sicknesses of the sensory system

Neurodegenerative infections influence different exercises that the body perform, for example, equilibrium, growth, speaking, breathing, etc. The majority of them are genetic. The causes can be smoking, cancer, or a cerebrovascular attack (CVA).

Neurodegenerative infections can be huge or perilous. It relies upon the sort. There are no treatment for a large portion of them. Treatment can help someone to avoid manifestations, mitigate torment, and increment versatility.

- *Parkinson's disease*

Other names: Parkinson's disease, Parkinson's, Parkinsonism, Paralysis with tremor

It a type of movement disorder. It occurs when nerve cells (neurons) do not make enough of a vital chemical in the brain known as dopamine. A few cases are hereditary, yet most don't appear to happen between individuals from a similar family.

Side effects start gradually, as a rule on one side of the body. Then they affect both sides. Some are:

- Trembling in the hands, arms, legs, jaw, and face
- Stiffness in the arms, legs, and trunk
- Slowness of developments
- Balance and coordination issues

As symptoms worsen, people with the disease may find it difficult to walk or do simple tasks. They may likewise have issues like discouragement, rest unsettling influences, or trouble biting, gulping, or talking.

There is no demonstrative test for this infection. Specialists utilize the patient's set of experiences and a neurological test to analyze it.

There is no cure for Parkinson's disease. Various medicines sometimes help substantially to improve symptoms. In severe cases, surgery and deep brain stimulation (electrodes implanted in the brain that send pulses to stimulate the parts of the brain that control movement) can help.

- *Alzheimer disease*

The most well-known illness in type of dementia in more current individuals is Alzheimer. We can define dementia as a cerebrum problem that seriously influences an individual's capacity to do their everyday exercises.

Alzheimer's beginnings gradually. It first influences the pieces of the mind that control thinking, memory, and verbal. Someone with the disease is relative to forgetting things, and even the names of their family.

Over time, Alzheimer's situations get worse. It may be difficult for them to talk, peruse, or compose. They may neglect to recall how to brush their teeth or brush their hair. Later on, they may bounce tense or exceptional or meander away from home. At long last, they need complete consideration. That can be unpleasant for relatives who should deal with them.

The common age of suffering Alzheimer is after 60 years. The risk increases as the personages. The risk is higher as it is genetic.

No treatment can stop the disease. A few medications can help keep indications from deteriorating temporarily.

4. Diseases of the blood vessels that supply the brain, such as _strokes_

- _Strokes_

Other names: Stroke, CVA, Stroke, Stroke, Cerebral infarction

A stroke happens when blood stream to some portion of the mind stops. When the brain does not receive oxygen and nutrients, the cells begin to die within minutes. That can cause severe brain damage, permanent disability, and even death.

Let's mention two:

- Ischemic stroke is brought about by a blood coagulation that squares or plugs a vein in the mind. It is the most well-known sort, 80% of strokes are ischemic

- Hemorrhagic stroke is brought about by a vein breaking and seeping in the brain

Another condition like a stroke is a transient ischemic outbreak. Sometimes it is called a "mini spill." It happens when the blood supply to the brain block for a short time. While the damage to brain cells is not permanent, it does put you at higher risk for a stroke.

5. *Spinal cord* and *brain injuries*

☐ *Spinal cord trauma*

The spinal cord is a bundle of nerves that runs down the center of the back. It transmits signals to and from your body and brain. Spinal cord trauma disrupts these signals. Generally, spinal string wounds start with a blow that breaks or disjoins the vertebrae, the hard circles that make up the spine. Most wounds don't cut the spinal string. All things being equal, they cause harm when parts of the vertebrae break the spinal tissue or push on the nerve parts that convey the signs.

Spinal cord injuries can be complete or incomplete. In a complete spinal cord injury, the cord cannot transmit messages below the level of that injury. As a result, the patient is paralyzed below the level of trauma. In incomplete trauma, some movements and sensations preserved below the injury.

☐ *Traumatic brain injury*

Other Names: Traumatic Brain Injury, Traumatic Brain Injury

It is an abrupt physical issue that makes harm the mind. It can happen from a blow, effect, or shock to the head. That is a shut head injury. It can likewise happen when an article enters the skull, which is known as an infiltrating injury.

Manifestations of a brain injury can be gentle, moderate, or extreme. Some of them are Concussions. Sometimes the effects can be significant. But most people make a full recovery. A more serious traumatic brain injury can lead to severe physical and psychological symptoms, coma, and even death.

6. Seizure disorders, such as *epilepsy*

- *Epilepsy*

Epilepsy is a brain problem that makes individuals have repeating seizures. Seizures occur when groups of nerve cells (neurons) in the brain send the wrong signals. People may have strange feelings and emotions or behave in unusual ways. They may have vicious muscle fits or pass out.

Epilepsy has numerous potential causes, including infection, cerebrum injury, and unusual mental health. Despite this, in many cases, the cause is unknown.

7. Cancer, such as *brain tumors*

- *Brain tumors*

Other names: Brain cancer, Brain cancer, Brain tumor

A tumor in the brain is a development of strange cells in its tissue. Tumors can be benign (not cancer) or malignant (with cancer cells growing very fast).

8. Infections such as *meningitis*

- *Meningitis*

Meningitis is aggravation of the meager tissue that encompasses the mind and spinal rope called the meninges. There are a few sorts of meningitis. The most well-known is viral meningitis, which happens when an infection enters your body through the nose or mouth and goes to the cerebrum. Bacterial meningitis is phenomenal, yet it might be deadly. It conventionally starts with microorganisms that cause flu like defilements. It can cause a stroke, deafness, and cerebrum harm. It can likewise harm different organs. Pneumococcal diseases and meningococcal contaminations can cause bacterial meningitis.

It is more normal in individuals with vulnerable immune system. It can deteriorate rapidly. You should look for guaranteed clinical consideration on the off chance that you create:

- A sudden fever
- Strong headache
- Neck stiffness

It can prevent with early treatment.

Things to avoid, Debunking Myths

Specialists advise keeping the brain well exercised and, in a certain way, shielding it from the constant deterioration that it suffers due to free radicals, pollution in cities, stress, and bad eating habits. Taken together, they represent a risk of neurodegenerative diseases or memory loss in adulthood.

- ☐ Don't suffer unnecessarily. Don't rust. Life is as it is
- ☐ Rest well and try to nap. Learn about how you breathe during sleep
- ☐ Move, walk. Do moderate aerobic exercise without going overboard
- ☐ Make the purchase right. Eat what is necessary.
- ☐ Drink water frequently and follow a diet low in salt, low in saturated fat, little meat, and rich in whole grains, nuts, vegetables, greens, fish, and olive oil. Try not to consume industrial pastries or processed products
- ☐ Avoid toxic relationships
- ☐ Do not smoke
- ☐ Moderate your alcohol intake, 1 beer/red wine a day. Don't get high
- ☐ Watch your blood pressure and your heart. Do not beat more than necessary

- ☐ Be careful with your migraine, especially if you tend to clot, take contraceptive treatment, or smoke

- ☐ Avoid hormonal contraceptives, especially if you smoke, suffer from a predisposition to your blood clotting, or have had miscarriages

- ☐ Be careful with chronic infections. Take proper dental health, get vaccinated against the flu if you have risk factors

- ☐ If an immediate family member has suffered a stroke before the age of 65, check yourself

- ☐ If you suffer from a sudden deficit in brain function, go as soon as possible to a hospital equipped with the "Stroke Code." If the symptoms are chronic, inform your trusted neurologist

CHAPTER TWO

MAINTAINING MEMORY

Memory allows you to save memories, knowledge, skills, and experiences that you live. In the study and at work, it is vital to use memory to retain data necessary for projects or exams. For this reason, it is vital to keep your memory in a great condition. In this chapter, I will show you some habits, games, and tricks to help you maintain your memory.

The ten habits to maintain memory

Habit #1: A healthy diet

Eating a good diet allows your brain to handle the energy it needs for a good memory.

Habit #2: Do exercises

Doing any sport helps oxygenate the brain and circulate better blood. You can accomplish something as basic as a 30-minute stroll to something all the more requesting like combative techniques.

Habit #3: Avoid stress

In spite of it sounds practically inconceivable, figure out what are the reasons for pressure in your life, and attempt to isolate yourself. You can do yoga or reflect to bring down feelings of anxiety.

Habit #4: Get involved

You are with your loved ones, friend, or even meeting new people helps memory. Remembering faces, data, conversations, and topics is a great exercise.

Habit #5: Do new things

If you want, you can learn something new, as cooking, or learning Russian. It will allow you to exercise your brain and have other skills.

Habit #6: Use an agenda

The memory will always need support, and nothing better than taking notes. It is good to put all the relevant information in a calendar so as not to lose it.

Habit #7: Travels

Living new experiences helps exercise memory. It will help you exercise your memory to remember something in the past. Also, travel help combat stress.

Habit #8: Read

A book opens the doors to different worlds, new situations, and helps to cultivate our imagination.

Habit #9: Do simple memory exercises

Try to remember birthdays without the help of Facebook, don't check your address book for phone numbers, or try to remember the names of the streets where you drive.

Habit #10: Look at the little details

Have a look at things, learn their shapes, the details that make them unique, and try to remember them.

You can exercise memory daily with good habits. There a lot of things you can do using technology. Take advantage of it. There are game apps that can help you speed up your memory.

Exercises to maintain and keep your memory active

We can exercise our minds while solving crosswords, sudoku puzzles, or just doing a nice puzzle. It's about our brain struggling to solve small mental challenges while having fun.

Mental training helps prevent mental illness and memory loss that we mentioned in the previous chapter. That is why it is so important to do this type of exercise.

Exercise #1: Find out which figure is missing on the left of the image

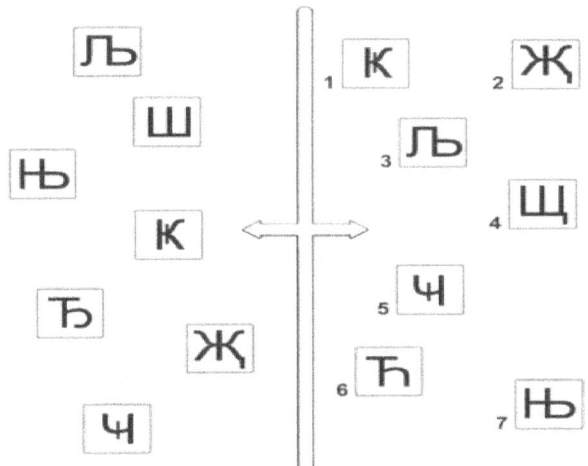

Answer: Figures 4 and 6 are not on the left side of the image as they have been modified.

Exercise #2: Find out which figure is missing to the right of the image

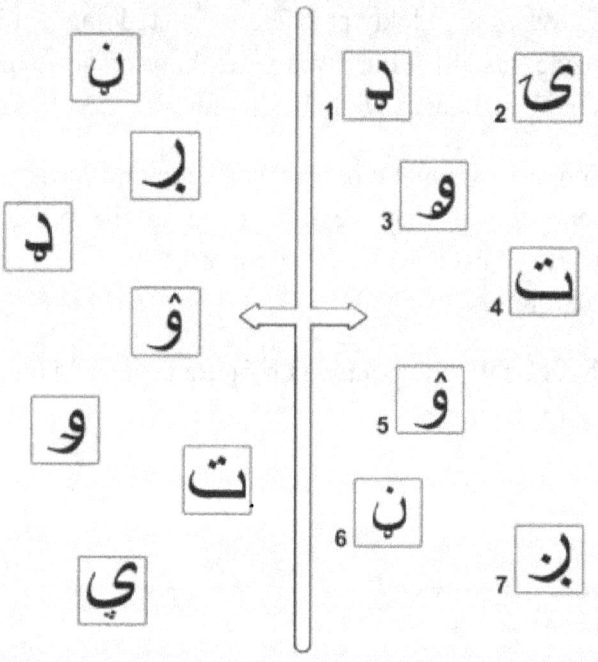

Answer: the figures that are not there are 2, 3 and 7 since they underwent modifications.

Exercise #3: Perform the following calculations. What results do you get?

    3.1. Add the larger numbers and subtract the small blue

3.2. Add the green numbers and subtract the sum of the red ones

3.3 Add the smallest size numbers and subtract the largest blue

3.4 Add the numbers on the right side and subtract the sum from those on the left

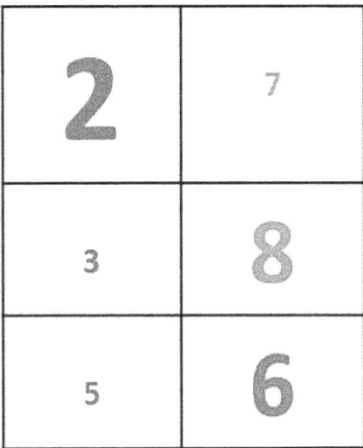

Results: 3.1 = 11 / 3.2 = 6 /3.3= 13 / 3.4 = -11

Exercise #4. Perform the following calculations from the assigned numbers:

7125

1-Add the first and last number ....

2-Add the second and fourth numbers ....

3-Add the third, second and last number ....

4-Add all the numbers and subtract 7 ....

5-Add the first three numbers and subtract the last one ....

65947

1-Add the third and fifth numbers ....

2-Add the last four numbers ....

3-Add the three highest numbers ....

4-Add the three numbers in the middle and subtract the last one ....

5-Add all the numbers and multiply by two.

....

3961

1-Add the first three numbers ....

2-Add the second, the last and the first number ....

3-Add the two numbers in the middle ....

4-Subtract the highest number from the lowest number ....

5-Add all the numbers and subtract 5 ....

Answers: **7125** (1 = 12, 2 = 6, 3 = 8, 4 = 8, and 5 = 5), **3961** (1 = 18, 2 = 13, 3 = 15, 4 = 8, 5 = 14) and **65947** (1 = 16, 2 = 25, 3 = 22, 4 = 11, 5 = 62).

Exercise # 5. Find out how many times each of the following pairs are repeated.

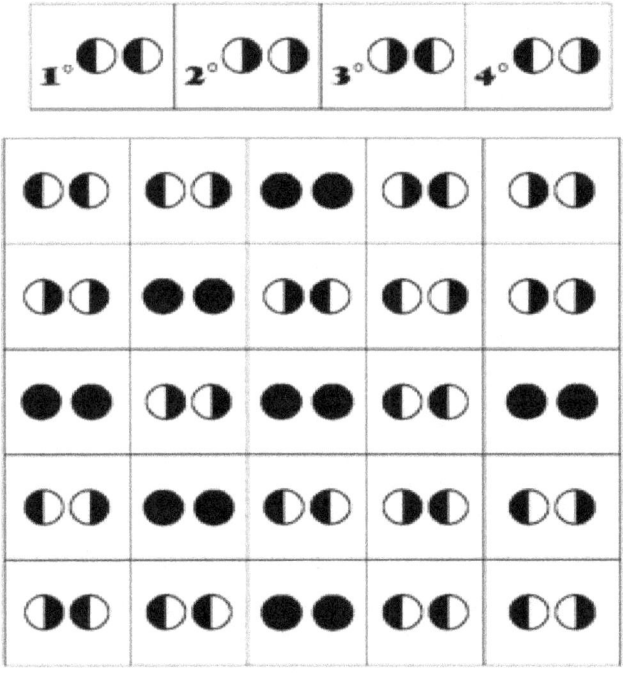

Answer: 1 = 5 times / 2 = 4/3 = 4/4 = 5

Tricks to maintain and keep active the memory

Trick #1: Open and close hands

That trick is available to everyone. Research carried out by the University of Montclair (USA) and published in the journal Plos One[1], revealed that clenching the right fist for 90 seconds helps in the process of memory formation. On the other hand, clenching the left fist also facilitates the retrieval of information stored in our memory.

Trick #2: Using mind maps

Making mind maps and learning them is a successful technique that allows for quick learning. For this, it is necessary to make diagrams with balloons that start from the same center, from which useful information gave to memorize.

Trick #3: Focusing on a topic that attracts your attention

Remembering lessons in subjects that one liked in primary or secondary school is normal. With the same criteria, as an adult, you have to look for

---

[1] https://www.medicalnewstoday.com/articles/259678#1

activities that interest you when storing new information.

Trick #4: Betting on a binary model

Make a mental film with new data to power the memory. For this, it is vital to make ridiculous affiliations, even with words not utilized as affronts or obscenities. It permits separated mental information stockpiling.

Trick #5: Learning to play a musical instrument

Teaching music through a new musical instrument stimulates a few cognitive abilities such as motor control, hearing, and memory.

Trick #6: Associate facts with images

When one thinks about something and fixes it with an image, better results are achieved by remembering that specific fact. Associative memory achieves better brain function.

Trick #7: Meditation

An investigation carried out by the University of California in Santa Barbara (USA) showed that with two weeks of training in what is known as "mindfulness[2]", it is conceivable to essentially improve understanding perception, the memory magnitude of work, and focus. Meditation is, therefore, a powerful tool to help us strengthen our memory.

Trick #8: Scribbling

When you scribble frequently and associate them with certain things helps to retain information and increases mental capacity and memories or memory. You can use basic geometric shapes such as lines, triangles, rectangles to form a visual alphabet in the mind that helps to remember.

Trick #9: Socialize

Relating to others, whether they are friends, family, or acquaintances, has been associated with a better memory. That is attested by a study by Australian researchers published in the Journal of Aging

---

[2] Zeidan F., Johnson S. K., Diamond B. J., & Goolkasian P. (2010). Mindfulness meditation improves cognition: Evidence of brief mental training. Consciousness and Cognition, 19, 597–605. 10.1016/j.concog.2010.03.014. Available at: https://pubmed.ncbi.nlm.nih.gov/20363650/

Research that showed that those participants who had greater contact with close friends, an important social network, had better performance in memory tests after a follow-up of 15 years.

CHAPTER THREE

CONCENTRATION

Concentration is the process through which we select some stimulus from our environment. We focus on a stimulant from among all those around us and ignore all the others.

Although it may seem strange, it occurs through reasoning. It consists of focusing our attention voluntarily on a specific aspect and being able to maintain it.

Dispersion	It occurs when you are aware of too many things and want to cover everything, with which in reality you do not pay enough attention to anything	To overcome this difficulty, organization is very useful.
Distraction	Concentrate on one's own stimuli (thoughts, sensations), which prevents attending to external stimuli (study).	In this case, it is useful to repeat yourself, as many times as necessary, that later there will be time to think about what you want but that now is study time.
Fatigue	It negatively affects concentration.	Rest is the most convenient solution.

Lack of foundation or knowledge	Necessary to understand what you have to study (if you do not understand what you read, for example, it is very difficult to maintain an adequate level of attention).	It will be necessary to dedicate time to review the basic contents and strengthen them.
Not knowing how to study		Knowing and applying study techniques helps to overcome this difficulty.

10 Exercises to Improve Concentration

It is much more fundamental and beneficial to perform tasks in a concentrated way than to do them with distractions. So, to improve your concentration, you have to follow the steps that we are going to give you below.

1. Get organized (Self-discipline)

It is the first thing you must do. It is more than an exercise that push you improve your concentration. It is vital to if you want to have concentration.

For this, there are two different aspects:

- *Distraction-free environment:*

Even if you trained well your concentration, concentration in an environment full of stimuli that can distract you. I will be impossible to focus as much as possible on the task you want to do.

Before starting, try to have an orderly environment without distractions: keep the door closed, the mobile phone silent, your favorite internet pages closed, etc.

- *Tasks structure:*

Do you want to focus? Do you know what you are doing? The order? And the way? The way you apply that concentration to tasks will be less helpful. It is not a concentration for a specific activity.

Before starting, write down on a piece of paper the tasks you think you can do, how, and the order. So, you can utilize that concentration in an organized manner.

2. Do not focus on two things at a time

One of the issues that frequently keep us from being able to think that we might want is having various considerations in our mind and not having the option to zero in on only one.

When it occurs, our capacity to focus reduces since our brain does not design to focus on many activities or thoughts.

Acquire a capacity for focus and to apply that capacity to concrete events, and eliminate various ways of thinking.

To obtain this capacity to separate a particular idea, an activity that can help us many is the accompanying: Sit in a seat, and when you are loose, among all the contemplations that ring a bell, pick just one.

The idea you pick can be anybody. For instance, the visit you had with your associate today, the photographs your niece indicated you a week ago, or the soccer match you saw on Sunday.

Whenever you have picked it, go through around 5 minutes considering everything and that's it. If you do this exercise regularly, you will get used to concentrate on only one thought.

3. Relax

Our states of worry, tenseness, or if we are not calm when performing a task are those that hinder our ability to concentrate.

It is advisable to be relax and avoid excessive stress to concentrate. As soon as you realize that pressure or uneasiness meddles with your capacity to focus, perform the accompanying profound breathing activity:

- Sit in a comfortable position, close your eyes. Put your right arm on your abdomen

- Breathe in through your nose and breathe out through your nose or your mouth

- Take 5 seconds of slow breath in through your nose. Maintain the inhalation for 5 to 7 seconds. Release the air for 10 seconds

- [ ] While you breathe, think the tension that escapes through the expired air.

- [ ] Repeat this exercise for 3 times.

- [ ] After completing, move to precise respiration: breathe in through the nose, at least 3 seconds and breathe out for other 3 seconds, but release the air

4. Use the numbers

One of the psychological exercises that most reinforce your concentration is count. To play out this kind of mental activities requires a degree of core interest.

Thus, in the event that it is hard for you to focus, rehearsing these exercises in your available chance to the most awesome aspect your capacity will improve your capacity to think.

There are a huge number of figuring exercises to do, and every one of them will be compelling in improving your focus as long as you do them circumspectly.

From doing the renowned sudokus that for some, individuals can be a more agreeable method of doing this sort of movement, to doing any numerical activity routinely, your capacity to focus will improve.

5. Train your attention

Concentration is an intellectual action intended to concentrate on a particular angle, another utilitarian activity is to prepare your attention.

So, having more prominent power over your attentional cycles, it will be a lot simpler for you to focus. Quite possibly the best approaches to work your consideration in your extra time is to do the common Wordsearch.

For example, before this Wordsearch, try to mark with a pencil:

- All the number 4's you find
- All the letters T you find
- All the odd numbers you find
- All the vowels you find

```
5 R 4 T 6 F 5 D 4 E 6 R 5 4 T 6 6 E 5 R 4 T
6 R 5 E 4 R 6 T 5 E 4 R T E 6 R 5 4 T 6 I F
A S F F 4 F 6 A 5 S 4 F 6 A 5 S 4 Q W E 5 R
4 T 6 Q 5 W 4 R 6 Q 5 W E 4 R 6 Q 5 W I
R Q 3 W 2 E I R Q 3 W 2 I R Q 3 2 W I 5
I T A 5 4 S 6 F 5 A 4 F I A 3 B A 3 B A B 4
C 4 D 5 E F 4 G 6 5 H 4 Y 4 J U 6 5 I O 4 P
6 L I O 5 I U 6 5 Q 5 E 4 R T 4 U 5 I 4 O 4
K 4 J 4 Y U 4 O 4 L 5 I 4 O 5 L 4 K P 4 4 O
5 I 3 O 2 I Ñ 3 K 4 L 4 A 5 S 4 I F D E 5 R
4 F I B I C 5 D E 5 R 4 F 4 E 5 R 4 A 6 S 5
E 4 R 6 E 5 R I F 3 A 2 S I F 3 A 2 I F 3 A
2 Q 4 W 5 E 4 R 6 T 5 R 4 T 4 Y 4 U 5 I 4
O 4 L 4 K 4 J 2 M I N H 2 Y 4 J 4 U 5 I 4 O
4 L I K 3 K 5 K 4 L 6 Y 5 U L 4 Y 9 U 8 I 7
O A S 5 D 7 4 F 4 E 6 R 5 T 8 G 7 R E 5 R
```

Once done, write down the time taken to complete the four tasks.

6. A moment of mindfulness

It is a Mindfulness strategy (care) that you can do whenever of the: prior day going to work, while hanging tight for the transport or when you enjoy a reprieve at the workplace.

The activity comprises of zeroing in on your relaxing for a few minutes, and its objective is to assist you with reestablishing your considerations, unwind and acquire that psychological lucidity that you may have been losing during the day.

To do this, you need to stand up, leave your eyes open, inhale with your tummy (not your chest), oust the air with your nose and concentrate on the sound and cadence of your relaxing.

It is practically sure that in the event that you do it, you may have different contemplations. At the point when this occurs, put forth an attempt to restore your thoughtfulness regarding the breath and disregard different upgrades.

It is an activity that is simple. It doesn't need a lot of time. Perform it in those snapshots of stress when you need clearness of thoughts or feel confounded about something.

7. Conscious observation

This activity, similar to care, is additionally a Mindfulness procedure. It is anything but difficult to rehearse. Also, it can help you a ton in improving your capacity to think.

For this situation, cognizant perception comprises of picking any article. Whatever you discover: a glass, a pen, or some tea.

Whenever you have picked the article, you ought to notice it cautiously and concentrate on it for around 3 or 4 minutes.

This basic exercise is exceptionally practical as it breaks the daily schedule of your brain. On the off chance that we take a gander at it, for the duration of the day, we see numerous things. We notice some with pretty much consideration. However, we once in a while notice something in a 100% cognizant manner.

Thusly, our psyche liberates itself from certain musings, centers around the present, and gives us a sensation of "being alert" that encourages us center around a specific angle.

8. The mental image

Mental image is another one that is very fundamental for the conscious observation.

Similarly, as with the other exercise, pick any object you have nearby (a pencil, a fork, a few shoes) and notice it, concentrating on it. What's more, attempt to recall everything about that object.

After observing well, use your mind to recreate an image. That image has to be similar to the item.

With this activity, aside from concentrating on the present as in the past one, you will chip away at your data stockpiling measures, so you should complete additional fixation work to recuperate the data from the article you have recently noticed.

9. Expression of our memories

Attempt to consider your recollections, that can give you delight. And yet, it requires a serious level of focus to have the option to recuperate the data that is in your mind.

At the point when you recall, aside from practicing your memory, you are by implication preparing your concentration. Presently, you should review in an organized and nitty gritty way. It does not merit pondering past occasions without concentrating on them.

Subsequently, an activity that you can do is recollect your vacations, recording all the subtleties that you recall about them: where they went, who you went with, what places you visited, what tales occurred, and so on

This activity should be possible around evening time, in a loose and quiet way, for around 30-40 minutes prior to resting.

10. Focus on your day

Another activity that you can do prior to resting is to attempt to recall all that you have done for the duration of the day when you hit the hay.

It is a straightforward exercise that requires basically no exertion, and it is fundamental to do it every day. Start doing this activity prior to nodding off.

You can do it when you are lying-in bed, and the goal is that during the 5 or 10 minutes that you do this activity, you can recollect with however much detail as could reasonably be expected all that you have done during the day, the individuals you have seen or the things that have grabbed your eye.

CHAPTER FOUR

SELF-LEARNING

Self-learning is the way of learning for oneself. It is acquiring knowledge, skills, values, and attitudes, which the person performs on his own, either through study or experience.

A person that focuses on self-learning searches for the information himself and carries out the practices or experiments in the same way.

Principles of self-learning

1. Definition of what we want to learn:

- ☐ Define the project by giving it a name. It makes you specify what you want to learn and not get lost in the abstract. And it also helps you to set limits in your learning

- ☐ The objective must be very particular, and that you can meet. For example, instead of setting your goal to play the guitar, let the intention be to play a specific song. In this way, you do not set an abstract

- ☐ Define the limits of your learning. Self-learning has a big problem. That problem is to learn everything about a subject. So, the solution is to set flexible limits that you will modify in the future

- ☐ The goal you set should be hard enough not to get bored and unchallenging enough not to give up. You have to strike a balance

2. Collection of material:

- ☐ Choose good material. One of the substantial challenges in learning something is knowing how to filter all the information we have and keeping only the first level material. The reason is that we have a lot of resources in this information age

- Complement materials of different supports. Do not limit ourselves to books, for example, but complement it with self-contained video courses, audios, etc. So, the combination of all these resources facilitates the establishment of concepts

- The problem will never be the lack of information, so the limit is on you. It is vital not to get overwhelmed with all the material that you find

- Once collecting all the material and filtering them, organize all the information, and create your agenda

- If you are ever going to pay for a resource, try to try it first

3. Establish a system for evaluating what has been learned

- It is essential in any self-learning you evaluate everything you have learned from time to time. Without this stage, you will never know if your methodology is working. For example: if you are learning Russian, spend a day trying to read a text, speaking during that day only in the language you want to learn. In this way, you will know if you are meeting your objectives

- These self-assessment mechanisms have to lead you to your final goal. That is, if you have planned to learn to play a song with a musical instrument, the guitar, for example, the test will be to try to play a part of that song in a time frame that you have set and see how your progress is going

4. Planning

You already have everything: resources, your defined evaluation mechanisms, etc. Set up a schedule. For this, different approaches are depending on our initial motivation and the size of our project:

- Daily plan. For sizeable objectives, this is the best type. It consists of dedicating a little time to our goal every day. It doesn't have to be a lot, for example, an hour to start. We must continue with this schedule that we set ourselves long enough to create a habit

- Obsessive plan. It consists of dedicating all your free time to the goal that you have set for yourself. It works for objectives that are not very big, or when your initial motivation is very high

5. What never to do:

- ☐ Do the project when you feel like it
- ☐ Not setting a schedule
- ☐ Not establishing self-evaluation mechanisms
- ☐ Not meeting the schedule

Traditional learning vs self-learning

Traditional learning occurs in a classroom setting. For it, a tutor will be available to moderate and regulate the flow of information and knowledge. So, the teacher expects the student to deepen their understanding through written exercises at home. Today, in self-learning, the students search for the information themselves and carry out the practices or experiments in the same way. However, in face-to-face instructional settings, the primary source of information is still the teacher.

What are the differences between self-learning and traditional learning?

If you are deciding between self-learning or traditional learning, it may be useful to consider the following differences:

Table

Self-learning	Traditional learning
In any moment, in any place	Forced to a time and place
Flexible pitch	Imposed step
Alone	Together with your colleagues
Supports an independent learning style	Learning from and with each other
Limited interaction	Extensive interaction between coaches and colleagues
self-learning	Traditional learning

These are the undeniable contrasts. However, there are not different regarding expenses and investment rates. Let's expand these points a bit:

Costs

Organizing traditional learning is valuable, but also expensive. Self-learning is often cheaper than the first one. Why? You don't have to deal with added costs like travel costs, training facilities, hiring a trainer, or printing training materials that come with face-to-face training. In 2019, training costs in the United States reached $ 83 billion! Of this money, 29.6 billion was spent on these additional costs. The structural expenses to operate online training programs are much lower.

Are there any similarities?

Despite there are a larger number of contrasts than likenesses between these restricting learning techniques, what they share for all intents and purpose is that they are both compelling.

Effectiveness

We cannot say that self-learning is more effective than traditional learning, or vice versa. It certainly depends on the subject of learning and how its effectiveness has been measured. But overall, it seems that self-learning is a fully developed alternative to classroom training. There is ample and good evidence that students generally learn as much self-learning as they do with traditional learning.

And the winner is…?

We'd love to pick a winner, but we can't. It would not be fair to either method of learning because both have their pros and cons. The correct learning method for you depends on many factors:

- ☐ What is your budget?

- ☐ What is the learning topic? Is it based on practice or knowledge?

- ☐ What do you want to achieve with the learning? Improve skills or update for a company standard?

- ☐ How much time do you want to spend learning? And how long can you spend in learning?

- ☐ What is the level of your motivation?

Possibly picking one over the other is excessively unbending. If you want to combine the best of both worlds, then you should seriously consider combined learning.

How to create a self-learning plan?

You cannot plan happiness. The reason is that you do not know what to expect in the next step. But when it comes to self-learning, most of the success depends on the ability to plan. So, when your plan is clear, you have more control over the entire educational process. Also, see how close you are to the expected result.

1. Objective setting

The objective of the task is to create a list of the knowledge you will learn. To do this, you need to understand the end goal and divide it into several components, for example, the lessons. It is called strategic planning: you think about each class in detail and decide what you want to achieve at the end of each one.

Then move on to tactical planning. The idea of this is that you think very carefully about what you will do in each lesson. You should discover and deal with the data fundamental for the class, learning, and test errands, and useful activities.

2. Determination of time

The task of the second stage is to allocate the time that you plan to allocate for self-learning. Initially, the total amount of time to spend on all training must determine, for example, six months. Then you should be guided by the points of the plan, which have been outlined in the previous stage.

For example, if you are sure that the necessary material will be mastered in 360 hours, it will turn out that you need to study 3 hours a day 5 days a week. That is, 3 hours*5 days = 15 hours*4 weeks = 60 hours*6 months = 360 hours. Reverse calculations can be done in the same way, but you need to know exactly how long it takes to master the material and how long you generally have.

For example, if you know that you have six months, and that the material will be learned 100% in 360 hours, you will have: 360 hours/6 months = 60 hours per month/4 weeks = 15 hours per week/5 days (because 2 days of rest are needed) = 3 hours per day are needed to study.

In addition, it is very important to bear in mind that the time spent studying the material will also depend on the amount of information received.

3.Definition of the methods

The third stage is no less important than the previous two. Your task is to identify the forms and methods to be used in the training, as well as the sources of information (internet, books, tutorials, video or audio learning materials), devices and tools (PC, laptop, smartphone, notebooks, pens, markers, pencils) to be used for that purpose. But if the sources of information and tools are simple, it is worth mentioning the methods in more detail.

☐ *Teaching methods*

Traditionally, teaching methods are divided into three groups:

- **Organization methods**: These, in turn, can be differentiated:

  ➢ *Regarding the sources of knowledge*: practical, visual and verbal (in the case of personal learning, practical and visual are used).

  ➢ *By the nature of the acquisition of knowledge*: problematic, research, search, explanatory-illustrative and reproductive (in the case of self-learning, search, research, problem and its reproduction are used).

  ➢ *By the nature of the presentation and the perception of the material*: deductive and inductive (in the case of our study, the deductive is used).

- **Monitoring methods**: That refers to the way you will be monitoring your own learning. For self-learning it is recommended to organize self-assessments.

- **Stimulating methods**: It involves the application of a set of self-motivation measures for learning. Several types of incentives can be used, for example, after a productive week of classes, you can make a stop and disconnect two full days off, meeting with friends, going to the cinema or a recreational park, etc.

In addition to these methods, which are considered fundamental, there are auxiliary ones. These include:

Passive method. It generally involves a passive perception of the information, when, for example, a teacher explains the material to the students, controls the lesson process, and checks the degree of assimilation of the information by the students. But in this case, this method is not the most proper because we are talking about self-learning. The only way to use this method is to use audio and video materials when they are passive listeners or spectators.

Active method. In general, an active teaching method is the dynamic interaction of students with the teacher. In a self-learning situation, the active method finds its expression in independent data searching and processing, making notes, using mind maps, flow charts, etc.

Emotional self-regulation

Emotional self-regulation can be the ability to manage emotions. It is a process in which the subject is able to influence the type of emotion, as well as the moment and the way in which it is expressed. Thus, a set of deliberate and automatic processes take place that produce behavioral, psychological and physiological changes that favor the adjustment in the intensity and direction of our emotions. Having good emotional self-regulation implies being able to identify what happens to us, monitor its progress, and intervene in it so that it ends up disappearing.

In light of this definition, the significance of having this limit very much created is reasonable. It allows us to face all kinds of life situations that we want or do not involve a series of emotional experiences. Anything that occurs, we have a past enthusiastic state and, in view of the attributes of that occasion, our state can change emphatically or contrarily.

Emotional regulation strategies

There are many emotional self-regulation strategies, and each person, as long as they do it functionally and adaptively, can apply their own. However, the most frequent are the ones you will see below.

1. Suppression of thoughts

This procedure comprises, as its name recommends, in smothering the considerations that cause us uneasiness. Thusly, we look to change the enthusiastic state, leaving the unsavory circumstance and going to one, envisioned or genuine, that doesn't cause us such a lot of pressure.

For example, if we think of a negative comment made to us today at work, which puts us in a bad mood, the option is attempt to obscure our consideration by tuning in to music or envisioning a wonderful scene.

Despite this approach is very common, simple, and cheap, it is not effective in the long term. It indeed offers temporary relief, but normally the thoughts you were running from end up coming back stronger.

2. Emotional reconsideration

The strategy of emotional reconsideration, or reappraisal, consists of modifying how we interpret a situation to try to change the impact it has on our emotional state.

For example, Imagine that you fight with your partner and they separate, there is no doubt that you will feel negative feelings such as sadness, uncertainty, or fear of not finding love again.

Through reappraisal, we can rethink the circumstance, seeing its positive side. For example, in this specific case, we can see that breaking up with that person is progress since we no longer have a burden in our life that keeps us from creating as full and cheerful individuals.

Emotional reconsideration is one of the successful and adaptive inner self-regulation strategies. It is intermittent in psychological conduct treatment.

3. Cognitive distancing

Psychological separating comprises of taking an autonomous and impartial situation despite the passionate occasion or circumstance that upsets us. Thus, we can reduce its impact on our mental state, and it is easier to choose the answer we want to give.

It is intricate, but to achieve it, what is done is to refocus our emotional state, calm down, and think coldly about what kind of response we want to give. It encourages us to not try to settle on awful choices without giving it much thought.

How to improve this skill?

According to what we have mentioned above, emotional self-regulation is a defensive aspect for psychopathology. Also, to avoid problems at the social and work level. For example, having the ability to prevent our feelings from controlling us while arguing with the partner or with the boss are ways to avoid breaking up with our boyfriend or girlfriend or ending up unemployed, respectively.

Next, we will see useful ways to improve emotional self-regulation in childhood, adolescence and adulthood.

1.In the childhood

An ideal time to work on this ability is childhood, given how moldable children are and their ability to learn comfortably. Children cannot regulate their emotions so early. So, when you help them to manage them in the educational and social context. That will help them avoiding poor academic performance and having conflicts with other children.

Firstly, people should teach the children identify their feelings at all times. Children often have a lot of trouble being aware of their emotions. For this reason, practicing deliberately to realize it can be functional, always starting from a state of relaxation.

Ask them to express their emotions. No matter what they are anger, fear, and sadness. The idea is to make them express these feelings in a safe and controlled way, so that, when they come into real life, they can identify them and can manage them.

2. In adolescence

Although they have a greater capacity to recognize emotions than children, adolescents can also have problems mastering this capacity. It is because, despite having more cognitive functions, adolescence is a violent period, where emotions are on the surface.

An excellent way to make them aware of their emotions is to keep a journal or calendar of their emotions. In the diary, they can write how they have felt each day, stating what triggered the emotion, the reaction, and what done to control it, while on the calendar they characterize what they have felt with colors.

Both the schedule and the enthusiastic journal are utilized for the young adult to dissect his/her perspective back and pose inquiries.

3. In adults

Adult people have a lot more prominent ability to recognize their sentiments, in spite of the fact that there are consistently the individuals who actually don't have sufficient enthusiastic self-guideline.

Likewise, in adulthood, we play with certain advantages. One of them is: we, as adults, have full control over the emotions if they not so intense. The other is that as ups and downs occur less frequently, self-regulation is not a capacity that seems so useful at first, and we consider that, either by inertia or by avoiding unpleasant situations, we have the circumstances under control.

But despite these supposed advantages, we need to improve a lot. The main objective of emotional self-regulation is to control factors for all kinds of unpleasant situations.

These circumstances will include a compelling enthusiastic reaction, and how we react can be imperative. Learning to respond in a calm, cool, and responsible way can be what makes us enjoy a happy life, whether our partner is by our side, they fire us, or the disease worsens.

Believing that we are enthusiastic thrill rides and that unexpected occasions occur in life starts things out. It is challenging, but it is also an easily observable reality. How we feel may not change to the gravity of our fate, but the way we are going to live it can.

CHAPTER FIVE

ACCELERATED LEARNING AND SPEED READING

What if you could learn more effectively and efficiently and have more fun during the process? Accelerated learning and speed reading offer you this opportunity.

What is speed reading?

Concisely, we can define speed reading as a mental gymnastics technique that allows us to understand texts and written messages more quickly, and in turn, helps to increase our intellectual field.

Using the techniques of speed reading, it encourages the way toward understanding and quick fuse of information. Therefore, through speed reading, you can learn to read faster and understand what we are reading.

Speed reading suggests a cycle where another kind of association produced between the two halves of the brain, from this connection, a kind of brain film is projected with what you read, taking full advantage of the mental field of each person.

The traditional method usually includes three fundamental steps: first, the information can visualize through individual syllables, then those syllables are phonetized into words. Firstly, the message is integrated into the cognitive field. On the other hand, the speed-reading technique consists of integrating these three steps into one, with which a general visualization of the information is imposed from the beginning through the perception of whole words and phrases.

Speed reading is a technique, and achieving your goals requires a lot of practice and systematic training. It is vital to establish a work routine based on the specific objectives of each person. Generally, the objectives tend to be: increase reading speed, increase comprehension capacity or increase concentration capacity when reading.

Speed reading techniques

There are straightforward techniques that can help you step on the gas when reading a document. Let's dive into them quickly.

#1. Relax

Find a suitable place for your reading. You need comfort, although not too much because good posture and good lighting are also necessary. Sitting in front of a desk is a great option, as long as the desk is neat and clean. With this, you will avoid distractions.

#2. Don't read aloud

Don't whisper either. What's more, don't move your lips. Many people believe that reading aloud works to improve concentration, but it depends on a great environment. When you read aloud, what you are doing is repeating what you have already read. So, you better learn to listen to your inner self and save reading aloud for when you read to someone else.

#3. Chase the words

You can use a pencil or toothpick to guide your reading. The goal is for your eyes to 'reach' the words you point. This simple exercise will dramatically increase your reading speed. Practice a lot and push your eyes to the limit. Try to go faster and faster and discover the maximum point where you do not sacrifice retention of words. You will surely be surprised.

#4. Group the words

With this technique, you will make small jumps from one group of words to another. Start by dividing sentences into groups of three or four words, and with some practice, you could be reading entire lines in no time just by briefly staring. To practice, you can use a marker to divide the sentences.

#5. Never go back

How many times do we go back a few lines higher or even go back to the previous page because we did not understand something important? That is a misreading. Learn to trust your eyes and yourself, and you will be amazed at your ability to understand much more than you think. So now you know: never, never, never look back. With this simple exercise, you will teach your brain to understand everything you are reading.

#6. Skimming technique

To locate keywords and to know the author's intention, the Skimming method seeks to quickly identify the main ideas, taking into account the first and last paragraph, as well as other elements of the reading such as the synopsis, highlighted sentences, summaries, among others.

However, it is not recommended as part of the study techniques since you can overlook a great explanation. It is used mainly to search for more specific information such as analysis of graphs, dates, or names.

#7. Fixation technique

Fixation is nothing more than the visual field in which we focus our attention when we read. The goal of this tactic is to decrease the number of fascination to achieve a successful reading.

What is accelerated learning?

The word "accelerated" refers to maximizing learning ability in a given time. Accelerated learning is not only related to time but also effectiveness. People learn more effectively in a positive and emotionally supportive learning environment.

Accelerated learning is about removing barriers to learning, and addressing outdated learning conditions, orchestrating information in a playful, multimodal, relaxed, positive, consistent, and coinciding way..

It is estimated that a normal person reads about 250 words per minute. If speed reading techniques are used, speed can be increased and between 400 and 700 words per minute can be read. The difference is notable, but the important thing is that the speed of reading also means comprehension of what is read[3].

Techniques for accelerated learning

1. Focus your attention on what you do:

For the processed information to move from short-term memory to long-term memory, we must focus on that information. Attention is one of the main components of memory, and that is why when we are studying it is essential that we find ourselves in a place where there are no distractions that disperse our attention.

Study technique: Find a quiet place where you can concentrate. It can be the library, your room. Put distracting items such as electronic devices out of your reach, and put them in silence. Avoid noise. You can wear earplugs if noise is unavoidable.

---

[3] Brysbaert, Marc, 2019/04/12. How many words do we read per minute? A review and meta-analysis of reading rate. Available at: 10.31234/osf.io/xynwg
https://irisreading.com/what-is-the-average-reading-speed/

2. Divide your study time into regular sessions:

People who study regularly retain information much better than those who have done study marathons a few days before the exam. If you leave everything to the last minute, you will overload your mind and make it difficult to process information. A short but regular study allows the brain to consolidate data and retain it for the long term.

Study technique: Study a little every day, and the day before the exam, review what you have learned. Create a study routine to make it easier for you. You can use reminders to remind yourself when you have to study. It may well be an alarm or reminders that act as clues. If you decide to learn every day after eating, food is the clue that will lead you to study. If, on the contrary, you say; "I will study for a while in the afternoon," you will not have any clue that leads you to study, and it is more likely that you will forget it.

3. Organize and structure your notes:

Scientists have shown that organizing information into groups that are related to each other helps us learn.

Study technique: Write your notes in a structured way. You group the concepts that are similar to each other. In this way, it will be easier for your mind to associate the related information.

4. Relate the new information to what you already know:

Relating the information to each other helps us to elaborate and integrate it, facilitating its learning.

Study Technique: When faced with new and unfamiliar study material, first think about how you can relate it to what you already know. By establishing relationships between new ideas and previously existing memories, you will remember the current information much better. Mind maps can also help you establish connections between concepts.

5. Visualize the concepts:

Visualization is a vital technique for memorizing concepts quickly.

Study technique: For this technique, your notes must be complemented with visual information. They can be photos, diagrams, and graphics. Underline them in different colors. Any visual aid that evokes the memory is valid.

6. Review aloud with another person:

Reading information aloud improves the memorization process. Many educators say that when students review aloud with each other, it takes less time to understand and remember new concepts.

Study technique: You can use this memorization technique by meeting with a classmate to study or ask someone in your family for help. If you can't find someone to help you review, you can recite the diary out loud to yourself. You can even use your stuffed animals as an audience. It may be a bit embarrassing at first, but many people find it helpful.

7. Prepare the information

Progressively elaborating and delving into a concept is a very efficient way to process information and encode it in long-term memory.

Study technique: You can start by reading the definition of the concept. By doing so, you will become familiar with it and then go deeper by reading expanded information about the term. Likewise, it can help you to find more information on the subject. For example, you can look for explanatory videos, talks, or documentaries that explain it differently and provide you with curiosities and anecdotes.

8. Change your study routine from time to time:

Breaking the monotony and getting out of the study routine can increase the efficiency of your memory and help you more easily retrieve information in the long term.

Study technique: You can try changing the place where you study. Or, you can change your review schedule. Nor do you need to make a radical change in your study habits try something new from time to time will be enough to relax your mind and increase your desire to work.

9. Find out what type of student you are:

There are several types of students with different peculiarities, some people have a greater attention span in the morning, and others have a more active mind at night.

Study technique: You have to know yourself well. Additionally, you should notice the moment wherein you exploit the examination to build up an audit plan. If you get up comfortable and get sleepy at night, you are more morning and probably concentrate better in the morning and early afternoon.

10. Write the concepts by hand:

We usually write our summaries on the computer, but it has been proven that writing things by hand helps to focus on the data that are most relevant and to synthesize the information, while if you write on your computer, you do not concentrate as much on what you are writing, doing it more automatically.

Study technique: Write several times by hand the concepts you want to retain. You can help yourself by creating summaries, diagrams of various kinds. Taking notes by hand can also help you to interpret and re-elaborate the information to memorize it more easily.

11. Don't listen to music while studying

Listening to music starts our brain activity, but it is not always beneficial. According to an investigation, any music distracts us and makes memorization difficult.

Study technique: A little while before you start studying you can try listening to some music to activate your brain. But when you begin to review, turn off the music. If silence bothers you, you can try putting on ambient sounds, such as birdsong or cafeteria noise.

12. Use the chain study technique:

This memorization technique is very functional and consists of matching the words of a summary and using them to create a straightforward sentence.

Study technique: For example, if you want to remember the elements lithium, beryllium, boron, carbon, nitrogen, oxygen, fluorine, and neon, you can create the phrase "The BBC doesn't work." You can also use this method to generate made-up words that make it easier for you to memorize content.

13. Take regular breaks

The breaks are fundamental to consolidate the information and that our attention recovers. You may think that you don't have time to rest, but the truth is that rest is the best investment you can make.

Study Technique: Planning your breaks depends a bit on how long you can hold your attention. Some people start to disperse after 20 minutes and others who can stay for a whole hour. The rest time should be proportional to the time you have been studying. If you study for an hour at a time, rest for 10 or 15 minutes. If you have been half an hour, 5-7 minutes of rest is enough.

If you have trouble taking breaks, you can try having a bottle of water with you. So, you can drink regularly. This way, you will need to go to the bathroom more often and force yourself to stop. You can take advantage of a turn or stretch your back.

You can also set alarms or use certain apps to remind you to stop and take a break.

14. Put the Leitner method into practice

The Leitner method is a very successful and interactive way of transferring the information we have to study from short-term memory to long-term memory. Also, it will force us to focus on studying more the information that is most difficult for us to learn.

Study technique: Divide the study material into cards or sheets by themes, concepts, or with the structure you want. And get 5 boxes (of shoes, for example). When you have all the chips, you put them in box 1.

The method consists of taking the cards out of box 1 and mentally evoking the information (we will tell ourselves the contents of the card. If we know it, we move it to box 2. If not, it stays in box 1. The objective is that on the first day, we proceed with all the chips to box 2.

Little by little, you will pass all the topics from box to box until you reach box 5. When you know them all, you will have to make a calendar to know how often you have to review each box. For example:

- ☐ Box 1: Review today
- ☐ Box 2: In one day
- ☐ Box 3: In two days
- ☐ Box 4: In a week
- ☐ Box 5: In a month

That plan has to be balanced so that you go through the box 5 days before the exam. If you do not remember a card well, it will return to the first box, regardless of the position it was in.

15. Take tests to practice

Doing exercises or mock exams helps us to test our knowledge and consolidate it better. Also, it will help us to know how we know the lesson.

Study technique: If possible, ask your teacher for sample exams or questions of the kind that will come up on the exam. Also, try to do the exercises that the textbook proposes.

16. Try the memory palace method

One of the most used memory resources is the so-called Memory Palace. This study technique can help you store a large amount of information in a structured way by creating fictitious sites in your mind. With practice, anyone can learn to use it.

Effective note taking

During classes, it is common for students to listen to the lesson and, at the same time, take notes that later allow them to study for exams and tests.

Students are used to writing down what they hear, but they should know that this is not the most effective method.

If you want to have better grades and understand what you study, you need to improve the way you take notes.

6 tips for effective note taking

1-Words, not phrases

Instead of writing everything as the teacher says, try to write down the most important words or ideas. You do not need to write down everything you hear, but rather listen carefully and write down the fundamental point of what it is trying to teach you.

2-Use your words

Instead of jotting down complex terms that you don't quite understand, use your words and transform your teacher's ideas into your ideas. This way, when you read them, you won't have to make an extra effort to understand them.

3-Use colors

You can create a whole system of colors, using one for the words whose meaning you need to deepen. Use another for the topics you must look for material. Use another for the most relevant ideas. In this way, you can also help your visual memory remember what you wrote down during class.

4-Divide the page

A great way to achieve more efficient notes is to divide the page into two spaces, or even three. The important thing is that in one, you write down the fundamental ideas of the subject. In the other, add the secondary ones. And, if you decide to add a third, you can leave it for those typical comments that teachers make that can later be used when studying, such as book recommendations in those who expand the information.

5-Schemes

When the topics are too complex, or even when they are historical topics that include antecedents, causes, consequences, and different aspects, it is best to take notes in outline form. This way, you will have an understandable way of relating each feature to the central idea.

6-Avoid abbreviations

Sometimes, motivated by the need to write down everything and that no idea escapes, we abbreviate words that we later do not understand. It is one thing to write the fundamentals. But quite another is to shorten each vocable until you get an incomprehensible text. Try to avoid abbreviations, and you will see how later you will understand your notes better.

Although at that moment it seems that the important thing is to "catch" all the ideas and capture them on the sheet, you must always remember that what is important is what comes next. How you read and learn these notes will determine your results in tests and exams you use this knowledge. Therefore, the most profitable thing is to learn to take successful notes from the first time.

Learning a new skill fast

There are no skills more difficult than others or more important. It all depends on the person. Some people find it easier to do physical activities, while others find it easier to do linguistic activities. The reality is that each of them has a particular value. Even things like being organized or working under pressure are principal skills that not everyone possesses. And you can learn it by targeting.

But can any skill be learned quickly? The answer is yes. So, let's see what you need to do it.

1. Focus on a single skill:

Although you surely want to acquire many skills in a short time, if you make it your task to learn all of them simultaneously, then it is very likely that you will have problems with each one and that you cannot become an expert in any of them. No brain can handle so much information!

If you want to say that you know how to do something, dedicate yourself exclusively to practicing one thing, and when you have advanced, it is the moment when you can start trying to learn the second skill.

Let your brain adjust to each one of them and give it space to dedicate the total effort individually.

2. Break down what you want to learn

You must define in detail what you want to do. And then analyze the elements and knowledge that make up this practice. Usually, what you want to learn is made up of various, more specific skills.

The more you break down the activity, the more you will decide which parts are essential for your goal. This way, you can organize yourself and define which skills to practice first. So, you can improve your performance.

3. Make time to practice:

It is impossible to learn a new skill if you don't spend time on it. Make sure to dedicate a minimum of 30 minutes to practice and learning each day. By doing so, the brain or body works to acquire mastery of a skill.

Even after you are a master at what you've decided to learn, practice a lot! So, you don't lose the progress you've made so far. Although the theory is vital, you should know that you need to spend more time practicing than reading theory.

4. Learn the little things that make up skill:

Each skill is from a combination of others. And an efficient way to learn is by dividing every little necessary thing into parts.

For example, if you want to drive a synchronous car, it is not recommended to be taught the mechanics of the pedals, the lever, and the steering wheel at the same time. Take your time to learn the speeds, then how to start, etc. So you can be clear about everything that constitutes what you want to achieve, and you can learn more easily and quickly.

5. Set a goal each week:

People work better when they know that they have a deadline. And that is why you should also set a deadline for your learning so that you can feel the need to comply. If you want to learn a new language, aim to learn 150 verbs in one week and learn greetings and goodbyes in another.

Practice, and while you are achieving the small goals, set a deadline to speak in the other language. Setting a deadline will motivate you to make learning part of your routine and take practice seriously.

What are you waiting for to get down to work and achieve what you set out to do? Your new and old skills will not only make you fun and proud, but they can also become a source of extra income if you wish.

CHAPTER SIX

TWELVE-WEEK PLAN TO IMPROVE MEMORY

There is no magic recipe that improves our memory with little effort. However, there are several exercises you can use to boost your cognitive abilities, and specifically, your memory.

In this section, we will find some that will allow you to develop new neural connections.

Week 1: Work on your focus

Tip: Start with short periods of concentration and gradually increase this time.

If you decide that you want to run a 5K race and need to get in shape, the worst thing you can do is start an extreme training program: you will end up hurt and discouraged, and you can quit before you start.

Similarly, if your attention span is short, the best way to develop it is slowly. Start with an easy goal and continue from there.

An easy way to start is by using the Pomodoro Technique.

Set a 5-minute alarm every day for a week. Focus on one task during this time frame. Then take a 2-minute break before refocusing for another 5 minutes.

Every day, add another 5 minutes to your focused work time, along with an additional 2 minutes to your rest time.

In 7 days, you should be able to work for 35 minutes straight before allowing yourself an 18-minute break. Once you feel comfortable with this method, you can work to lengthen your focus sessions a bit longer, while shortening your rest times.

Week 2: Conquer the distractions

Tip: Create a list of distractions to review later.

Because the Internet has made any information instantly accessible, we tend to look for something the moment it crosses our minds. "What will the weather be like tomorrow?" "What movies are they showing this weekend?" "I wonder what's new on my Facebook?"

The turn off your energy to get back to work since it takes us an average of 23 minutes to return to our original task, moving away from what we are working on the moment these questions or thoughts appear in our mind.

To solve this and not get distracted, whenever you have something to review, write it down on a piece of paper to look up later. Do that for a week while you are working on the previous point.

Once you have finished your focus session, or in your moment of rest, you can turn your attention to this list.

Week 3: Exercise your body

Tip: Aerobic exercise is substantial for the body and brain.

When you perform any exercise, it can affect the brain in multiple ways: it increases the heart rate that pumps more oxygen to the brain. Also, it encourages the body's arrival of a heap of chemicals. For that to be conceivable, it gives a sustaining climate to the development of synapses.

Start to integrate exercise in the third week. In this way, by coordinating a little aerobic exercise into your program, you can help your brain be more attentive. Physical activity, diet, and weight are factors that can contribute to overall functioning and concentration levels.

For example, if you skip breakfast, it is unlikely that before noon you will complete tasks and concentrate because you feel hungry.

Taking care of your health, staying active, and eating healthy foods is the best way to improve your concentration.

Week 4: Train your Visual Memory

Tip: Use exercises to work your visual memory during a week.

Visual memory is the ability to remember information you receive visually. We usually speak of immediate recall (4-5 seconds), of all the details of a visual element, and of being able to find these details from a selection of elements.

Describing an image: Choose the image you want and watch it for 30 seconds, trying to look at the details. After that time, remove it and answer these questions: what have you seen? What colors did the image have? and what different objects appeared in the picture? Finally, write a short story about the image.

Practice time: 2 consecutive days in a week

The review of the day: When you go to sleep, spend a few minutes recalling an event from that day. Try to provide all the information you remember: the people with their gestures and attitudes, if there were animals, the space in which the event took place, the light, the colors.

Practice time: 2 consecutive days in a week

The game of cuts: Choose a painting or photograph that you know a lot. Cut it into several parts and hide one. Try to reconstruct that part that is not visible. Make the exercise more challenging by progressively removing more pieces and mentally recreating more areas. You must be able to fill in a gap before removing more. The goal is for you to remember the image in your mind and great detail.

Practice time: 2 consecutive days in a week

The 3 methods to improve your visual memory when studying are easy to apply, and you will surprise with the results. In addition to serving for your exams, they can also be useful for other moments in your life in which you have to pull from memory. Rest the next day after applying the 3 exercises for 6 days a week.

Week 5: Train your Verbal Memory

Tip: Use Grouping, Categorization, Association, and Name Remembering as your main objectives to work memory this week.

Word Grouping: This game requires patience and good humor. You make a list of words. Try to have up to 4 categories, for example, car, traffic light, cat, cookie, banana, teacher, dog, apple, fish, bicycle, doctor. Repeat the list out loud 5 times. The goal is to remember as many words as possible. In turn, classify them by category.

Categorization could be: animals, professions, food and street objects. Using a pencil and paper is a good start. When you least expect it, you can mentally sort words.

Association technique: It is very functional when you want to remember or memorize words or objects.

You have to create a mental association relationship between the two words. Visualize that association for a second. The image must be instantaneous, do not last more than three seconds with that image. As in everything, practice is vital to improve memory and apply this technique every time you want to remember words.

For example;

To remember the following pairs of words:

Mirror – Bird: Visualize a huge bird looking or getting ready in front of a mirror. You can also visualize a mirror with wings flying like a bird.

Airplane – Ladder: Visualize a giant plane with a ladder tied to the top of the plane. It can also work to visualize an airplane going up some stairs.

Dog – Computer: Here it can work to imagine a dog using the computer or you can visualize yourself walking a computer on a leash similar to walking a dog.

Horse – Fish: You can visualize the horse swimming in a river or you can also imagine the horse fishing on the banks of a river.

You can make a list of 10, 15, and 20 words arranged in pairs. As you progress you can add more pairs of words every day until you reach a week.

Week 6: Try to memorize

Tip: Set a goal of memorizing what you did every day for the past 5 weeks.

Memorizing techniques, tips, or games that you carry out in the past is an effective way to make your brain more receptive to memory.

You don't need to try to memorize all the things you've done. Start from the first week. Try to recall the ones that seem most important to you.

This type of memorization task exercises your brain, giving it the strength to retain more information.

Some easy exercises to do are:

- Test your memory: Make a list and memorize it. An hour later try to see how many items on that list you can remember. Try making even more challenging lists for even more mental stimulation.

- Draw a memory map. After returning home from visiting a new place, try drawing a map of the area; repeat this exercise every time you visit a new location.

Week 7: A site for each thing and each thing on its Site

Every time you've just used something, put it back on your site. Every object has a home to which it belongs.

That is a traditional, minimal rule of personal organization. It is related to the saying: "Out of sight, out of mind." Anything that is out of the visual field is no longer a source of distraction.

Tip: Every day, try to put 3 things in their places. Do it for during a week.

Application

Look around you: what three things are not in place? Put them in their sites, and if they don't have one, find them "a home" and leave them there.

Remember: only three things at a time. No more. Not less. There is a justification for it.

Start small. It would be unaffordable if you tried in an afternoon to give a place to all the objects in your house. Start with a table or a shelf in the kitchen. Then, successively, day after day, continue to do it with the rest of the surfaces of your rooms - it is the place where more junk usually accumulates, and energy stagnates. It might take weeks. It's okay.

Observe and note the reduction in mental agitation. Enjoy the increasing calm created by a physical environment free of materials and distractions that allows you to focus on one thing at a time. This feeling will motivate you to continue. There will come a time when you wonder how it was possible that you ever lived in an environment full of things.

Week 8: Develop habits of visiting new places

Tip: Take at least 3 days a week to visit a different place.

Traveling is good to fill our hard drive with new and appealing data, through our own insight. Connecting with new societies, scenes, spots, and dialects present to us an irrefutable advancement and furthermore animates our interest, which keeps a cozy relationship with our memory and capacity to learn.

If you have enough resources to travel, do not hesitate to do so. Visit unknown places, immerse yourself in the culture and learn from the natives. If you can't travel so far, don't despair. Surround yourself with different people from different cultures. Meet people from other countries, and visit new places in and around your city.

For each place, you visit, try to have a summary of your journey through those sites. Vary the experiences in each one. Do something different each day.

Week 9: Learn a new language

Speaking two or more languages seems to be related to some protection against cognitive decline. In addition, in some studies it was found that bilingual people obtained higher scores in intelligence tests[4]. The interesting thing is that this happens, even when the language is learned in adulthood.

We advise you this week, start learning Spanish, French ... or whatever language it is. Practice with other colleagues and try to get along in social situations in a new language.

Week 10: Practice Meditation

Tip: Take 10-15 daily to practice any form of meditation during a week.

It has proven to be a good practice to improve the Speed of Mental Processing, Sustained Attention or Concentration, Inhibition, in addition to enhancing our memory and giving us better capacities for emotional management, among other things[5]. It is a

---

[4] de Bruin A, Treccani B, Della Sala S. Cognitive advantage in bilingualism an example of publication bias? Psychol Sci. 2014. 10.1177/0956797614557866. Available at: https://pubmed.ncbi.nlm.nih.gov/25475825/

[5] Lutz A., Slagter H. A., Dunne J. D., Davidson R. J. Attention regulation and monitoring in meditation. Trends in Cognitive Sciences. 2008;12(4):163–169. doi: 10.1016/j.tics.2008.01.005. Available at:

highly recommended practice for any mental athlete, as well as for people who want to improve their psychological health. The practice of yoga and meditation help us make more efficient use of our mental resources. They also reduce stress and anxiety, improving our performance.

How to do it: Today yoga and meditation are in fashion. It will not be difficult for you to find classes to learn.

Week 11: Walk backwards

Tip: It is obvious that you cannot do it being on the street. But take specific time for that every day. You can also do it in the exercise routine.

Perhaps this was not the exercise you had in mind to help your memory, but it has been proven to be tremendously effective.

A study recently showed that walking backwards helps to better remember events from the past[6]. Even better than walking forward or standing still.

---

https://www.ncbi.nlm.nih.gov/pmc/articles/PMC2693206/

[6] Aleksandar Aksentijevic, Kaz R.Brandt, EliasTsakanikos, Michael J.A.Thorpea. It takes me back: The mnemonic time-travel effect. Available at:
https://www.sciencedirect.com/science/article/abs/pii/S0010027718302658

In this study, participants who watched a video with objects moving backwards, or even imagined that they were moving backwards, remembered better.

The researchers dubbed it the "mnemonic time travel effect," and while they are still not sure how this relationship works in the brain, it could have real-world applications, for example for the next time you need to remember something.

Week 12: Reduce little by little the alcohol consumption

Tip: While eating every day, replace the alcohol for water, juice at your taste.

To keep your brain in top shape, you cannot drink more than 1 glass a day if you are a woman or 2 if you are a man (although this is related to weight and height standards so in your case it may vary). In general, a large alcohol intake is associated with greater memory loss[7].

Excessive alcohol consumption, even occasionally, can lead to hangovers that include dehydration. Since even mild dehydration can have a negative impact on

---

[7] Anstey KJ, Mack HA, Cherbuin N. Alcohol consumption as a risk factor for dementia and cognitive decline: meta-analysis of prospective studies. Am J Geriatr Psychiatry 2009; 17:542–555. Available at:
https://pubmed.ncbi.nlm.nih.gov/19546653/

mental functioning, limiting alcohol consumption can help prevent this.

Set that as a goal each day for the entire week. You will see that in a week, you will create the habits of not drinking too much alcohol.

CONCLUSION

Through our journey in this book, you have seen that memory is a mental process through which we preserve thoughts, skills, and experiences. If you keep the memory in good condition, you can avoid forgetting.

Additionally, there are day-by-day propensities that can help you keep your memory fit as a fiddle. And, we put them in the book for you. As that can show up in adulthood, it is better to prevent this problem before. So, the best way to prevent is to practice what we put in the book for you.

The memory allows linking knowledge of other subjects. If you strengthen this capacity, you will achieve great relationships between areas of knowledge and thus achieve greater complexity in your understanding of the different subjects in a global way.

Remember, remembering the happy moments of the past is an act of emotional intelligence that improves your health in the present to have a better quality of life.

www.ingramcontent.com/pod-product-compliance
Lightning Source LLC
Chambersburg PA
CBHW072206100526
44589CB00015B/2393